REVISED EDITION

MY VISIT TO THE DINOSAURS
by ALIKI

A Harper Trophy Book • Harper & Row, Publishers

for Marilyn Kriney

The *Let's-Read-and-Find-Out Book*™ series was originated by Dr. Franklyn M. Branley, Astronomer Emeritus and former Chairman of the American Museum–Hayden Planetarium, and was formerly co-edited by him and Dr. Roma Gans, Professor Emeritus of Childhood Education, Teachers College, Columbia University. Text and illustrations are checked for accuracy by an expert in the relevant field.

My Visit to the Dinosaurs
Copyright © 1969, 1985 by Aliki Brandenberg
All rights reserved. No part of this book may be used or reproduced in any manner whatsoever without written permission except in the case of brief quotations embodied in critical articles and reviews. Printed in the United States of America. For information address Harper & Row Junior Books, 10 East 53rd Street, New York, N.Y. 10022. Published simultaneously in Canada by Fitzhenry & Whiteside Limited, Toronto. Published in hardcover by Thomas Y. Crowell, New York.
Revised Edition
First Harper Trophy edition, 1985.

Library of Congress Cataloging in Publication Data
Aliki.
  My visit to the dinosaurs.

  (Let's-read-and-find-out science book)
  Summary: A visit to a museum of natural history provides a little boy with an introduction to the habits, characteristics, and habitats of fourteen kinds of dinosaurs.
  1. Dinosaurs—Juvenile literature. [1. Dinosaurs] I. Title. II. Series.
QE862.D5A35 1985   567.9′1   85-47538
ISBN 0-690-04422-4
ISBN 0-690-04423-2 (lib. bdg.)

  (A Let's-read-and-find-out book)
  "A Harper trophy book."
ISBN 0-06-445020-1 (pbk.)   85-42748

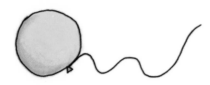

MY VISIT TO THE DINOSAURS

Yesterday I went to see the dinosaurs.
I went with my father and my little sister.
We walked down a hall, turned a corner—
and there they were.
Skeletons. Real dinosaur skeletons.
They were standing in a room bigger than a house.
One skeleton was almost as long as the room.
It looked scary.

My father told my sister and me not to be afraid.
Dinosaurs lived millions of years ago.
No dinosaurs are alive today.

I took a picture of the long dinosaur, APATOSAURUS.
Then I went over and looked closer.
The skeleton was wired together.
Heavy rods held it up.
I could see that some of the bones were not real.
They were made of plaster.
What a job it must have been to put
this huge puzzle together.
How could anyone know where all the pieces fit?

When dinosaurs died, they were covered with sand and mud.
They were buried for millions of years. The sand and mud
turned into rock, and the dinosaurs' bones became fossils.

In 1822 the first dinosaur fossil was found.
It was found by accident.
After that, many diggers went looking for fossils.
They dug in the rocky earth.
It is hard work to take fossils from the ground.
They are often embedded in solid rock.

The diggers found fossil bones of dinosaurs.
They found fossil eggs, which dinosaurs
had laid in sandy pits.

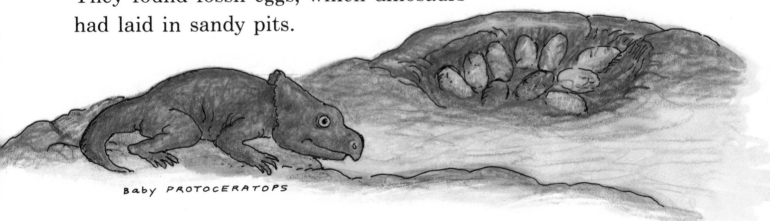

Baby PROTOCERATOPS

They even found fossil baby dinosaurs.

Paleontologists studied the fossils carefully.
A paleontologist is a scientist who studies animals
and plants of the past.
Paleontologists know when dinosaurs lived, and where.
They know what most dinosaurs ate.

CORYTHOSAURUS
(DUCKBILL DINOSAUR)
HERBIVORE

STYRACOSAURUS
(HORNED DINOSAUR)
HERBIVORE

ANKYLOSAURUS
(ARMORED DINOSAUR)
HERBIVORE

STEGOSAURUS
(PLATED DINOSAUR)
HERBIVORE

Some dinosaurs ate meat. They were carnivores.
Most dinosaurs ate plants. They were herbivores.

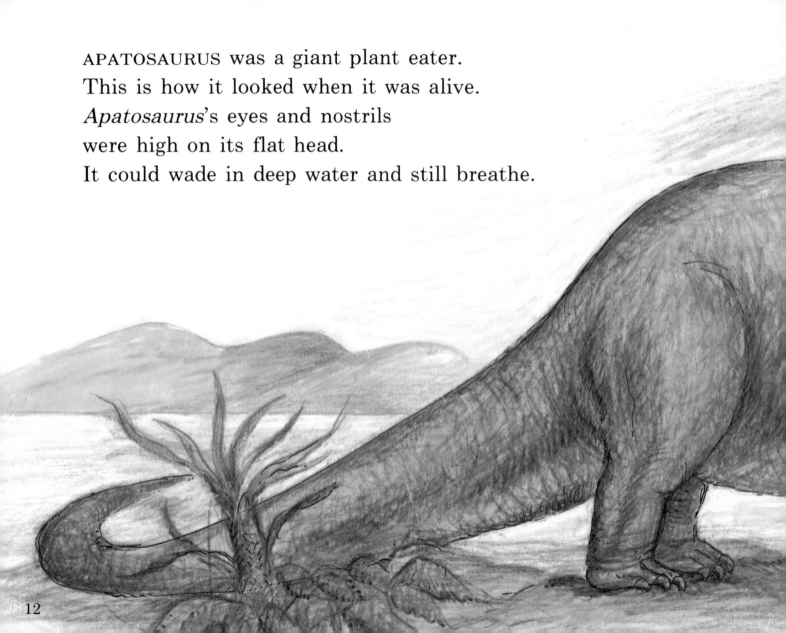

APATOSAURUS was a giant plant eater.
This is how it looked when it was alive.
Apatosaurus's eyes and nostrils
were high on its flat head.
It could wade in deep water and still breathe.

BRACHIOSAURUS was the heaviest dinosaur of all.
Some say it weighed over 100,000 pounds.
Brachiosaurus had a nostril on the top of its head.
It spent much of its time in swamps eating tons of soft, mushy plants.
But it laid its eggs on dry land.

DIPLODOCUS was the longest dinosaur of all.
It was 90 feet long from its tiny head to the tip of its tail.
It had a little mouth and just a few teeth.
Diplodocus had to eat almost without stopping,
in order to fill its huge body.

IGUANODON was a smaller plant eater.
It walked mostly on two legs.
It had spiked thumbs and a powerful tail
to swat its enemies.
Iguanodon had hundreds of flat teeth.
When one tooth wore out,
another grew in its place.

ANATOSAURUS was a duck-billed dinosaur.
It was a good swimmer.
Its front feet were webbed, and its "bill"
was shaped like a duck's.
It had more than 1000 teeth to crush and grind its food.

ALLOSAURUS was a meat eater.

Meat-eating dinosaurs were fast, fierce hunters.

Allosaurus ran on two strong legs.

It had dangerous claws and long, pointed teeth.

It ate any dinosaur it could find.

It was not even afraid to attack one twice its size.

My father, my sister, and I went to another hall
and looked at more skeletons.
There were so many to see that we had to hurry.

CRETACEO
DINOSAU
HALL →

CORYTHOSAURUS
DUCKBILL
DINOSAUR
BRAZIL

TRICERATOPS
HORNED DINOSAUR

ORNITHOLESTES was small and fierce.
It was swift enough to catch birds.

ORNITHOMIMUS had no teeth at all.
It may have eaten the eggs of other dinosaurs,
and fruit and insects too.

ANKYLOSAURUS was an armored dinosaur.
It lived on land and ate plants.
It had plenty of protection from meat eaters.
Who would want to bite its thick, leathery skin
covered with bony armor?

We saw STEGOSAURUS, a plated dinosaur.
It had big, bony plates down its back,
and a dangerous spiked tail.
Its brain was the size of a walnut.

We saw horned dinosaurs, too.
MONOCLONIUS had one horn on its nose.

STYRACOSAURUS had a horn on its nose
and a collar of spikes around its neck.

And TRICERATOPS had three deadly horns—
one on its nose and one over each eye.
A big fan-shaped bone protected its neck.
My father said *Triceratops* could defend itself
even against *Tyrannosaurus rex.*
I wondered who *Tyrannosaurus rex* was.

Then I saw it.

TYRANNOSAURUS was king of the dinosaurs.

And the fiercest of them all.

When it walked on its huge hind legs, the earth shook and other dinosaurs ran.

But *Tyrannosaurus* caught them, clawed them, and ate them with its long, sharp teeth.

I had to stand far away from TYRANNOSAURUS
to take its picture.
My father and sister looked tiny next to it.
I was glad *Tyrannosaurus* isn't alive anymore.
When you go to the museum, you will see what I mean.